Proper Care of the Centipede Lawn

Grow a Lush Weed and Insect Free Lawn

Stephen W. Stout

Proper Care of the Centipede Lawn

Copyright © 2009 by Stephen W. Stout

This book is dedicated to my partner, my mentor, my best friend, my wife. She is the most unselfish and openhanded person whose refining direction and principles are an inspiration to all.

Acknowledgments

I wish to acknowledge the support, both direct and indirect, in the research, writing, editing and publishing of this book.

- Southern Turf Industries
- The United States Department of Agriculture
- Tifton Seed Farms
- Lowe's
- Burgess Seed Company
- Perdue University
- University of North Carolina
- Clemson University
- The Ortho Company
- Wikipedia
- Nature's Lawn Company
- Gopher Software
- Word Press
- Book Design Wizard 2.0
- Create PDF
- Steve Low
- The Gopher Lawn Care Forum

Foreword

History of Centipede Grass in America

The history of Centipede grass in the United States can be traced back to Frank N. Meyer. Some literature refers to him as Dr. Meyer but I have not been able to verify the degree. He was at the very least an accomplished linguist speaking, reading and writing English, German, French, Spanish and Chinese. He was also an accomplished botanist.

Figure 1 Frank Meyer

Born Frans Nicholaas Meijer in Amsterdam, in 1901 at the age of 26 Dr. Meyer immigrated to the US. Grant Meyer began working at USDA's Plant Introduction Station in Santa Ana, California, where in 1904 David Fairchild (Chairman of the United States Department of Agriculture, Office of Foreign Seed and Plant Introduction), saw the greatest potential in Frank Meyer, and asked him to travel to East Asia in search of plants of economic value for the USDA. He was then introduced to Charles Sargent and instructed carefully on what plants had already been discovered, so he could avoid unnecessary duplication. At one time or another, both Sargent and Fairchild had planned to travel to China with him, but circumstances prevented it, and Frank Meyer went to China alone.

Dr. Meyer conducted four expeditions' to East Asia. 1905 to 1908, 1909 to 1911, 1912 to 1915, and 1916 to 1918. He collected tens of thousands of specimens, which represented approximately 2500 new plant introductions to the US. Among them were many notable crops such as soybeans, new types of grain, fruits, vegetables, bamboos, Chinese cabbage, Elms, bean sprouts, bamboo shoots and water chestnuts.

On his fourth expedition, the political environment in China was changing dramatically and in 1918, he decided to return to the US.

Unfortunately, bandits, before his return to the US, killed Dr. Meyer on June 1, 1918.

When his suitcases were returned, to the US a collection of various seeds was found including one small package of he called Chinese grass. That small packet was sent to the USDA Belle Glade Experiment Station near Savannah, Ga. under the name "Chinese Love Grass".

In the early 1920's A Quitman, Ga. Man, Jack Renfroe sent what was then renamed Centipede grass to four other experimental stations in Florida and Georgia. Four sprigs of the grass were found on the loading dock after the shipments were sent. Jack Renfroe's father, Riley Refroe, had a 400-acre farm near Quitman and he planted the three sprigs that survived in a 40-acre pasture.

Almost 30 years later, in 1950, Ray Jensen, a soil scientist with the USDA visited the Renfroe Farm to make a soil survey and noticed the Centipede turf. When Jensen left that evening, he left with some Centipede for his new home under construction in Tifton, Ga.

The next year, Jensen contracted with the Renfroe family to produce seeds from the 40-acre pasture he had developed from just three live sprigs of the Chinese grass, and Southern Turf Nurseries was born. Shortly after that, joined by his son-in-law Charles Rainey, he started Tifton Seed Farms.

That one small package of grass seeds from China sent to Washington, DC, by Dr. Meyer started an industry. Centipede lawns from seed, sod from seeds got their start in Tifton, Ga., and quickly spread throughout the Southeast, and then throughout the world.

Table of Contents

Centipede Grass

(Eremochloa Büse)

Figure 2 Centipede Range

Centipede Grass is a low, medium textured, slow growing, but aggressive grass that can produce a dense, attractive, weed-free turf. Since centipede produces only surface runners, it is easily controlled around borders of flowerbeds and walks.

Centipede grass has become widely grown in the southeastern United States from South Carolina to Florida and westward along the Gulf Coast states from South Carolina to Texas.

Its popularity as a lawn grass stems from its adaptation to low fertility conditions and its low maintenance requirements. Where Centipede grass is adapted and properly managed, it has few serious pest problems. It is particularly well adapted to the sandy, acid soils of the southeastern United States. Its westward movement is somewhat limited by severe iron deficiencies that develop in the alkaline soils of the arid regions. In addition, its northward movement is restricted by low temperatures. Extended periods of 5°F or less can kill Centipede grass.

Centipede Grass

Figure 3 Centipede Grass

Centipede grass is moderately shade tolerant, but grows best in full sunlight. Centipede grass thrives on moderately acid soils, pH 5 to 6. Above pH 7.0 iron becomes a limiting factor and supplemental applications of iron are required.

Centipede grass does not enter a true dormant state during winter months and is severely injured by intermittent cold and warm periods during spring. Hard freezes kill the leaves and young stolons of Centipede grasses. The grass usually recovers as soon as temperatures become favorable. Recurring cycles of cold / warm during the winter months depletes its energy reserves and is susceptible to extreme winterkill. Thus, its adaptation is limited to areas with mild winter temperatures.

Centipede is the ideal grass for the homeowner who wants an attractive lawn that needs little care. Centipede does not require much fertilizer or mowing, and compared to other lawn grasses, is generally resistant to most insects and diseases. It does, however, respond to good management and provides a very attractive turf. Centipede can be established from seeds, sprigs, or sod.

Centipede Cultural Data

Aeration	One of the secrets to a great lawn is having a porous, well-aerated soil where roots can grow deeply and biolife can thrive. According to the experts, the best soils should contain about 25% air. Unfortunately, most soils in this area have high clay content or are very compacted. They need to be loosened up and core aeration does not seem to do much to help. Natural Lawn Aeration contains a liquid soil penetrant that breaks apart tightly bonded clay particles. This creates "space" in the soil, allowing roots, water and air to permeate. We also add bio-activators (humates, seaweed and molasses) to help speed up your soil's regeneration. When the soil is well aerated and bioactive, roots grow deeper and plants are much healthier. The soil drains faster when wet, but it actually holds more water when the conditions are dry.
Brix Level	A Brix level of 12 or above will make lawn insect free
Drought Resistance	A strong centipede lawn will survive periodic droughts, but it will be more resistant to pests and other problems if you water it during dry spells.
Fertilization	Centipede grass needs low-nitrogen fertilizer without phosphorus or potassium. Fertilize in the spring and fall. Over fertilizing centipede with phosphorus causes changes in soil

	chemistry that make it impossible for the grass to take up iron, an essential nutrient for good green color.
Growth Rate	Centipede grass is slow growing
Humus Depth	Ideal Humus depth should be 4 inches or more
Ideal pH	4.5 to 5.5
Irrigation	A Centipede lawn will survive periodic droughts. Water only when dry spells last longer than two weeks.
Lawn Disease	Over watering will lead to lawn disease.
Mowing Height	Mow at 2 to 3 inches. Never mow too close when Centipede is not actively growing or you can invite problems with weeds. If the lawn is stressed by drought, mow less often and raise the mowing height to 3 inches.
N-P-K	Use only chlorine free organic 9-0-0 fertilizer.
Perennial Ryegrass Overseeding	Not recommended
Shade Tolerance	Centipede will grow in light dappled shade, but it grows most vigorously in almost-full or full sun.
Soil Type	Centipede likes slightly acidic soil aerated soil.
Sun	Centipede grass grows most vigorously in almost-full or full sun.
Thatch	If more than a 1/2-inch layer of thatch is present, (thatch is dead stems and debris that accumulates at the soil's surface, apply a liquid dethatcher. Mechanical dethatching is messy and less effective and takes away vital nutrients and Humus material. Biological Dethatcher is a liquid solution that has been formulated to generate and accelerate the decomposition of thatch in lawns. To fuel this process, high levels of thatch digesting bacteria and enzymes are incorporated. These,

	along with naturally occurring soil organisms, will break down thatch and turn it into valuable Humus.
Traffic Toler-ance	Centipede grass does not withstand heavy traffic.
Type	Centipede is a warm season grass.
Weed Control	Using a pre-emergent fertilizer weed suppres-sor such as Corn Gluten (9-0-0) in early spring will inhibit nearly all broadleaf weeds from sprouting. Centipede lawns when properly fed grow thick and weed free.

Proper Care of Centipede Grass

A Centipede lawn is not your typical lawn! Proper care and requirements are much different from that of other warm season grasses such as Bermuda, St. Augustine, Zoysia, and Fescue. Following maintenance procedures for those grasses will harm and even kill Centipede grass. Most workers at your local hardware and department stores do not know this and may steer you wrong.

Nutrients

Healthy Centipede grass requires more micronutrients than macronutrients (nitrogen, phosphorous, and potassium). Soil amendments should contain vitamins B-1, B-12, gibberellins, indoles, auxins as well as trace elements of boron, iron, zinc, cobalt, copper, manganese, molybdenum, and sulfur. These nutrients should be chelated, meaning they are instantly available to the plant. They should be salt and chlorine free to be safe to the grass and the soil.

Centipede Grass Deficiency Symptoms:

Nitrogen – Nitrogen deficiency is rarely a problem with Centipede Grass.

Potassium – Most grasses use potassium to build cells and tissue. Centipede grass however, is not like most grasses and handles potassium poorly.

Phosphorous – Phosphorous is harmful to the root systems of Centipede Grass. Micronutrients and trace elements handle this job in Centipede grass.

Plants require smaller amounts of secondary macronutrients –

6

Sulfur, calcium, magnesium, iron, manganese, zinc, copper, boron, and molybdenum and are essential for growth. They are often referred to as micronutrients or trace elements. Each of these serves specific purposes for our grass.

Magnesium – Centipede foliage will appear yellowish green with red edges. Even though it is classified as a secondary macronutrient, magnesium is still critical for growth. Without magnesium, plants cannot use sunlight to make food through photosynthesis! Plants also need magnesium to be able to take in other essential nutrients and to make seeds.

Calcium – New leaves will be small and grass will be rust colored. As with sulfur, Centipede grasses need calcium to make proteins. Calcium promotes new root growth and facilitates overall plant vigor (what potassium and phosphorous do for other grasses).

Sulfur – Fully-grown leaves turn yellow. One of the secondary macronutrients, sulfur helps plants maintain their dark green color. Mainly, plants use sulfur to create essential proteins. In Centipede grasses, sulfur is essential for nitrogen-fixing nodules and necessary in the formation of chlorophyll. Plants use sulfur in the processes of producing proteins, amino acids, enzymes, and vitamins. Sulfur also helps Centipede's resistance to disease, aids in growth, and in seed formation.

Iron – The new grass will turn yellow. Iron makes for healthy, dark green growth. As with magnesium, iron is essential for photosynthesis. Iron is necessary for chlorophyll formation and, without it; plants would not be able to carry out essential cellular functions.

Manganese – The new grass turns yellow. In short, manganese makes things happen. Manganese is necessary for chlorophyll formation, and without it, grasses would not be able to carry out essential cellular functions.

Zinc – Grass leaves will appear shriveling, narrow bladed and smaller than usual.

Boron – Yellowed grass and immature growth. Centipede grasses do not need much of it, but boron does facilitate nutrient uptake and it helps plants to grow new tissue.

Molybdenum – Fully-grown and mature grass appears grey-green. Centipede needs molybdenum to produce essential proteins.

Copper – Copper contributes too many natural processes including plant metabolism and reproduction.

Fertilization

Centipede grass needs a low-nitrogen fertilizer without phosphorus or potassium (9-0-0). Fertilizing with a nitrogen percentage higher than 9 more than twice a year will harm Centipede turf and promote lawn disease, weeds and insect infestations. I use a corn gluten fertilizer (a fertilizer but also a pre-emergent weed controller) in early spring and late fall. Do not use after reseeding until grass seeds have germinated (it will stop grass seeds also). There is no weed and feed product on the market other than corn gluten that will do more good than harm to Centipede grass.

Green-up

Do not use a nitrogen-based fertilizer to green up Centipede grass. It will harm the turf making it prone to disease, weed proliferation, and insect infestation. Centipede grass can be effectively greened up using lawn sulfur and/or iron. Both sulfur and iron will lower soil pH but Centipede's ideal pH is alkaline (a pH of 4.5 to 6.5) so there is little danger of lowering the pH too much. (Also, most broadleaf weeds cannot survive well with a soil pH lower than 7.0).

Irrigation

Irrigate Centipede grass only when the grass shows signs of moisture stress, such as off color, wilting or rolling leaves. If your Centipede shows footprints after walking on – irrigate. When you do water, you should water deeply! Apply water to wet the soil to a depth of 4 to 8 inches. This generally requires about an inch of water.

How do you judge an inch of water? I use empty cans such as vegetable cans (aluminum cans are too light and tip over easily). Place them at various places on the lawn to check sprinkler coverage. Periodically check the water level in the various cans with something as high-teck as a ruler.

Thatch

Thatch is a spongy layer of organic substance made up of leaves, grass roots and stems, rhizomes, and other similar materials that build up in your lawn. Excessive thatch accumulation has lead to lawn rooting into thatch rather than soil. Thatch will block water and nutrients from reaching your grass's roots, weakening the whole plant. Thatch can also trap moisture near the blades of your grass, increasing the likelihood of lawn disease.

Thatch Layer in this pic is very matted and about 2" thick! Aeration is needed.

Figure 4 Lawn Thatch - Perdue University

The primary component of thatch is turfgrass stems and roots. It accumulates as these plant parts buildups faster than they do breakdown. Thatch problems are due to a combination of biological, cultural, and environmental factors. Cultural practices can have a big impact on thatch. For example, heavy nitrogen fertilizer applications or overwatering frequently contributes to thatch, because they cause the lawn to grow excessively fast. Avoid over fertilizing and overwatering. Despite popular belief, short clippings dropped on the lawn after mowing are not the cause of thatch buildup. Clippings are very high in water content and breakdown rapidly when returned to lawns after mowing, assuming the lawns are mowed on a regular basis (not removing more than one-third of the leaf blade). As thatch levels accumulate to greater than 1/2 inch, lawn problems may begin, and the thatch needs to be controlled. Thatch may be torn out with a dethatcher, vertical mower, or with a bio-enhanced liquid dethatcher.

Biological Dethatcher is a liquid solution that has been formulated to generate and accelerate the decomposition of thatch, green organic matter (grass clippings), brown organic matter (leaves and twigs) in lawns. To fuel this process, these products contain high levels of thatch digesting bacteria and enzymes killed off by chemical and synthetic fertilizers. These, along with naturally occurring soil organisms, will break down organic matter and turn it into valuable humus (fertile soil) very quickly making for a plush healthy lawn.

Due to recent advances in liquid biological dethatchers, I no longer use the mechanical dethatcher or vertical mower to remove thatch from the lawns I service because I have found the biological dethatcher to be more economical, much more effective, and with much less mess. The only drawback I have encountered is storage of unused dethatcher. It is biological with living organisms and must be stored in a controlled environment between 41 and 78 degrees F.

Aeration

Aeration has both long and short-term major benefits:

- Promotes air exchange between the soil and atmosphere reduces soil compaction deeper, healthier root growth
- Improves nutrient uptake and use decreases water runoff and puddles
- Conserves water by improving soil water uptake
- Makes the turf more heat and drought tolerant
- Enriches surface soil improving resiliency and cushioning
- Promotes healthier more drought resistant lawns due to increased rooting.
- An increase in microorganisms in the soil. A healthy population of microorganisms will help break down any organic matter (thatch) and help by discouraging any lawn diseases
- Enhancing water infiltration from rainfall and irrigation reduces soil compaction improves soil structure and humus formation
- Increases earthworm activity
- Helps bioactivate all soils
- Improves rooting by loosening soil
- Improves air and water penetration
- Improves drainage & prevents erosion

Along with mechanical dethatching, mechanical aeration is now outdated. Liquid aeration is the present and future of lawn aeration. It is less expensive, more effective, easier to use, and safer to use for sprinklers, tree roots and buried electrical lines. I no longer use heavy mechanical aeration equipment. I have found liquid aeration results far superior in every aspect.

It is non-toxic, safe to handle, good for the lawn in many ways, and easy to apply.

Compacted soils cause unhealthy plants, lawns and trees. They stay soggy when wet, and turn rock hard when they dry out in the summer. When soils are "tight", necessary air, water and nutrients cannot move through the soil. Disease occurs. Roots are stunted. Beneficial microorganisms cannot survive. Plants are stressed and weakened. When you are doing everything else right, soil compaction will ruin all your efforts.

Comparison

Action	Mechanical	Liquid
Ground penetration	1-3"	6-12"
Soil structure	Unchanged	Dramatically changed
Coverage	Cores every 6"	100% Coverage
Water infiltration gain	15-35%	60-85%
Timing	When ground is saturated	Any time
Equipment	Heavy machine	Garden hose and sprayer
Time for improvement	4-6 weeks	Immediate
Thins lawn	Yes	No
Enhances weed growth	Yes	No
Harms pipes, sprinklers, tree roots, buried wires	Yes	No
Mess	Leaves messy lawn plugs	No mess
Soil conditioner	No	Yes

Lawn Mowing

Proper mowing is one of the most important practices in keeping your lawn healthy. Grasses are like most plants — if you clip off the growing points (the tips of the stems where the new leaves develop), the plants branch out and become denser, which in this case, turns thousands of individual grass plants into a tightly woven turf or a lawn. If you did not mow at all, your yard would look more like a prairie than a lawn. However, the mere act of mowing is not what makes a lawn look good. Mowing height and mowing frequency determine how healthy and attractive your lawn looks.

Aside from zoysia grass, Bermuda grass, and centipede grass, most other lawn types do not require frequent mowing during the spring and fall. Certainly no grass should be scraped down in the hot growing season in summer. First, when you cut any grass, you reduce the total blade area of the plant. Maintaining an ample surface of blades helps your lawn handle the grasses' essential photosynthesis, helps block weeds from germinating, and contributes to a hearty root system.

Taller Grass Can Be Beneficial

In addition, ample blade surface contributes to the green appearance of the lawn, absorbs water and nutrients, and helps your soil maintain moisture. Most experts agree that you should not cut more than a third of your total grass height at any one time.

You want to mow your lawn a little higher during summer stress months. For example, fescues, Kentucky bluegrass, and ryegrasses should be mowed to between 2 and 2.5 inches in spring and fall and 2.5 and 3 inches in summer. And alter the direction of the mowing from the last time. Changing angles and directions helps prevent grass from lying over. Higher mowing heights in the summer help keep soils cool and retain vital moisture at the roots.

Benefits:

- No need for you to buy, replace, or maintain expensive equipment

- Gives you more time for other more important things

Centipede Decline

In mature Centipede grass lawns (3 or more years old) problem areas sometimes appear in the spring and grow worse throughout the summer. These problem areas usually develop in thatchy turf, compacted soils, drought areas or areas under other stresses. Since a specific disease organism has not been identified as the cause, the problem has been broadly named "Centipede decline" and is used to describe the most common problems observed on Centipede grass. These include dollar spot, large patch, fairy rings, nematodes, ground pearls and nutritional problems.

Symptoms: the grass gradually deteriorates and is replaced by weeds or other invasive grasses. The grass often greens up in early spring, but gradually turns off color, wilts and dies. These areas resemble Centipede-grass suffering from drought conditions.

Examination of the turf in these areas reveals little root development. Many of the stolons, or runners, have no root attachment to the soil. Some small discolored roots may be found in the thatch, or the organic layer. The grass may be dead in the center of the discolored area with often-dark green, leaves radiating into the healthy grass.

Dollar spot is a disease that is often seen on centipede grass during the summer. The symptoms of this disease are light brown spots 2 to 4 inches in diameter. It does not appear to cause serious damage. Centipede grass that is declining because of other factors may have more dollar spot than nearby healthy grass. The grass may continue to decline in the affected patches, especially in dry weather, for a long time after the disease activity has stopped.

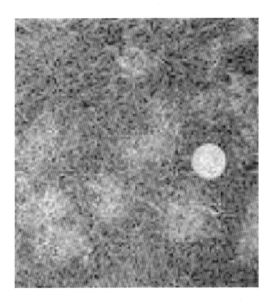

Figure 5 Dollar Spot - Perdue University

Figure 6 Fairy Rings - Perdue University

Fairy ring symptoms are large circular dead spots, dead rings, or green rings (3 to 20 feet in diameter) that enlarge for several years. Mushrooms of the fungi that cause this disease may be present at the edge of the rings or throughout the circles sometime during the year. Mushrooms may not develop for several years and suddenly appear following a weather pattern that induces mushroom development. Effective treatments are not known for fairy rings in lawns, however, rototilling the soil and replanting healthy grass has eliminated the problem in some cases. Adding iron supplements have also eliminated the problem in some cases.

Note: Mushrooms not in a circular pattern are not a sign of Fairy ring. Mushrooms often develop over dead tree roots as part of the natural decomposition process.

Sting Nematodes

Sting Nematodes have been associated with the decline in sandy soils in some cases. The sting nematode has been shown to cause very serious damage on Centipede grass in sandy soils in the Carolinas. Centipede grass affected by this nematode will become Thin and even die during hot-dry weather. Incorporation of organic matter in the soil may help overcome nematode damage; however, care must be taken to avoid too much nitrogen being released for Centipede grass.

Figure 7 Ground Pearls - Perdue University

Ground pearls are small scale insects that attack the roots of Centipede grass and may cause circular dead areas that resemble fairy ring. The spots enlarge each year and only weeds grow in the spots. Ground pearls are identified by the presence of small pearl-like bodies on the roots or in the soil. The pink adult stage that crawls is present during early summer. A control is not known for the ground pearls. Other types of grass, such as Bermuda grass or Bahia grass, appear to be less sensitive to ground pearls and should be considered for lawns with severe ground pearl problems.

Nutritional factors, including low potassium levels in sandy soils, high phosphorus levels, the use of too much nitrogen fertilizer, and low or high soil pH (5.5 is best) have been associated with the problem. High soil pH will cause Centipede grass to turn bright yellow, especially in the spring, due to iron deficiency (iron chlorosis). High phosphorus levels can increase iron chlorosis since it can replace iron in the plant. The use of fertilizers high in phosphorus may contribute to the decline of Centipede grass. High nitrogen caused the stolons to be above the soil where they are more susceptible to damage by cold weather. More centipede decline usually occurs in the spring and summer following very cold winters or following winters with unusually warm weather and then late cold periods. Excess nitrogen reduces cold and drought tolerance of Centipede grass. Potassium may help to reduce stress during the summer and winter.

Centipede grass is not very drought tolerant and is damaged during very dry weather. Irrigation when needed will help reduce damage from drought stress. Localized dry spots of soil that are hydrophobic (difficult to wet) have been associated with declining patches of Centipede grass. The soil in these patches needs extra aeration.

The use of chemical/synthetic herbicides (as sprays or in fertilizers) has been associated with the decline problem. Once a good stand of Centipede grass is established, weeds usually are not a problem because of the allelopathic activities that Centipede grass has against other plants. Therefore, herbicides should not be needed on Centipede grass if it is managed properly.

Centipede grass is not very shade-tolerant and does not grow well under trees with dense foliage. Root competition from nearby trees may increase drought stress and sometimes causes fairy ring like symptoms. The landscape should be redesigned to use mulch or shade-tolerant groundcover plants in these areas if the trees cannot be removed.

Centipede grass will usually spread over dead areas more rapidly if the old grass is removed and the soil loosened (aerated). New sprigs or overseeding in the areas will facilitate faster recovery.

Control: Cultural practices provide the most effective means of preventing centipede decline.

Brix

You're Lawns Brix Value

So, What Exactly Is Brix?

Brix is often referred to as the "sugar" or sucrose content of a plant or the produce from it, but this is a very simplistic and incomplete view of Brix. In actuality, Brix refers to the total soluble solids (TSS) in the juice of the produce or sap of the plant. Total soluble solids refers not only to sucrose (sugar) but also to fructose, vitamins, minerals, amino acids, proteins, hormones, and other solids found in the plant, fruit or vegetable.

The higher the TSS or Brix value, the healthier and more nutrient/mineral rich the plant is.

How Does a High Brix Help Me With My Lawn?

A liver is necessary to digest sugar. If an insect, which does not have a liver, ingests sugar, that sugar will eventually turn to alcohol and kill the insect. Insects instinctively know this, and plants with high Brix value (and, as a result, high sugar content) will emit different UV light patterns and electrical charges which communicate to insects that they should stay away.

Unfortunately, it has become the norm to ignore those warning signs and simply kill off all the bugs - either with some toxic chemical or with some natural alternative. Of course, of those two options, the natural insecticide is certainly the better option, but it still does not address the central problem of this situation. The bugs are there for a reason. The plant is not healthy. Make the plant healthy and the sugar content of the plant will rise, the insects will move on to a more attractive food source.

Grass Has a Brix Value Too

The higher the Brix value, the higher the sugar content. Therefore, the higher the Brix value of your grass, the more likely it is that insects will not be feasting on your lawn (if they do, they will die trying).

In fact, a Brix value of 12 or higher is all it takes to eliminate most insect infestations of any plant, including a lawn. Brix values for many grasses can reach values well over 20 or 30.

I use a 0 – 32 Reflectometer and find most lawn Brix values of 3 – 6, some at 7 – 9, and very few at 10 – 12. I have found none above 12! The length, amount and time of chemical and synthetic fertilizer use greatly negatively affect the Brix value.

Figure 8 Reflectometer

Most grasses have such low Brix value (typically no greater than about 6 or 8 and often much lower) that insects will feed on them all day long Raising the Brix of a plant is really quite simple. Provide good nutrition, including a balanced diet of macro and micronutrients and trace elements. Organic fertilizers and soil amendments such as humic acid will provide much better nutrition to any plant than chemical fertilizers will. Some fertilizers will raise Brix values more effectively than others will. For instance, kelp fertilizers are probably the most effective means to improving the overall nutrition of any plant (and, therefore, the Brix value) because most kelp fertilizers are made from Kelp grown in very cold, virtually toxin free and nutrient dense waters, such as the North Atlantic. Since kelp is a plant itself, the macro and micronutrients it provides are completely balanced and easily available to a plant. Thus, the addition of kelp to any fertilization program is probably the easiest way to increase the Brix value of that plant, which includes grass. Therefore, adding regular doses of kelp to your lawn care and landscaping fertilization program will increase the Brix of your grass and plants. The higher that Brix value gets the less insect and disease problems you will have. if you have any sort of insect problem, it is a fact that your lawn is receiving very poor nutrition, and is, therefore, very sickly, even if it doesn't necessarily look sick at this particular moment. Improve the nutrition the plant is receiving and the bugs will move elsewhere.

Soil is the Soul of Your Lawn

Decades of synthetic fertilizers, pesticides and compaction have all but made South Carolina lawns sterile!

Humus is degraded organic material in soil, which causes some soil layers to be dark brown or black. In soil science, humus refers to any organic matter that has reached a point of stability, where it will break down no further and, if conditions do not change, remain essentially, as it is for centuries, if not millennia. Humus has a characteristic black or dark brown color, which is due to an abundance of organic carbon. Chemically stable humus is the layer of fertile soil grasses need to flourish.

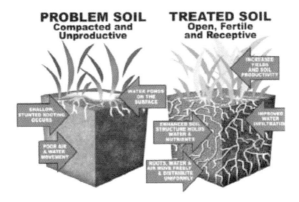

Figure 9 Problem Soil - UNC

The ideal lawn will have a humus layer up to 10 inches deep. Most South Carolina lawns have a layer of only about ¾ inch. Humus transmutes sterile dirt into fertile soil. Derived from organic matter of all kinds, humus is the life support system of the soil. The presence of humus among mineral particles and air spaces enables soil to nurture plants two ways. Humus creates a loose structure that simultaneously holds moisture and drains well. Humus also creates an environment that supports living organisms that convert soil nutrients into a form plant roots can use, building soil fertility. In short, humus brings soil to life.

Years of applications of synthetic fertilizers and pesticides have made your soil biologically sterile. The number and activity of microorgan-isms in the soil is depleted. High salt fertilizations programs reduce humus count to less than 2%. Synthetic fertilizers and pesticides make your lawn green but they also turn your lawn into "a junky" that always need more. A green lawn is not necessarily a healthy lawn.

Benefits of soil organic matter and humus

- The mineralization process that converts raw organic matter to the relatively stable substance that is humus feeds the soil population of micro-organisms and other creatures, thus maintaining high and healthy levels of soil life. The rate at which raw organic matter is converted into humus promotes (when fast) or limits (when slow) the coexistence of plants, animals and microbes in terrestrial ecosystems Humus can hold the equivalent of 80–90% of its weight in moisture, and therefore increases the soil's capacity to withstand drought conditions.
- Effective and stable humus are further sources of nutrients to microbes, the former providing a readily available supply while the latter acts as a more long-term storage reservoir.
- Humification of dead plant material causes complex organic compounds to break down into simpler forms, which are then made available to growing plants for uptake through their root systems.
- Humus is a colloidal substance, and increases the soil's cation exchange capacity particles (the degree to which a soil can adhere to and exchange cations. Soil particles and organic matter have negative charges on their surfaces. Mineral cations can absorb to the negative surface charges or the inorganic and organic soil particles. Once adsorbed, these minerals are not easily lost when the soil is leached by water and they also provide a nutrient reserve available

to plant roots); thus while these nutrient cations are accessible to plants, they are held in the soil safe from leaching away by rain or irrigation

- The biochemical structure of humus enables it to moderate — or buffer — excessive acid or alkaline soil conditions.
- During the humification process, microbes secrete sticky gums; these contribute to the crumb structure of the soil by holding particles together, allowing greater aeration of the soil. Toxic substances such as heavy metals, as well as excess nutrients, can be che-lated (that is, bound to the complex organic molecules of humus) and prevented from entering the wider ecosystem. The dark color of humus (usually black or dark brown) helps to warm up cold soils in the spring

Carbon compounds make up 50% of humus itself. The carbon compounds contained in the humus are used by microorganisms through the process of fermentation and respiration, converting it into high-energy values used by the plant for growth. Other portions of the carbon may be spent, or used in the oxidation of mineral compounds into simpler and more available forms of energies. Humus as a concentrate of carbon and energy compounds, aids bacteria to survive excessive moisture, cold or dry conditions. Humus enables bacteria to carry out antibiotic effects in the soil, as well as aiding bacteria interrelations with plant roots.

Humus absorbs the highly active non-nutrient hydrogen sources present in the soil and makes them immediately available as a food source for assimilation and usage by the plant. The humus colloid, or particle, will absorb and hold three times more mineral cations, water, and carbon compounds in the soil that are in a readily usable form for the plant to utilize. The humus colloids also protect (buffer) the microbial and plant systems against excessive sodium, magnesium, potassium, as well as other positive charged minerals, as the humus colloid carries a negative charged ion. The humus colloid also acts to buffer and enhance the four basic anions: carbon, nitrogen, phosphorous and sulfur, in their system of nutritional service to the soil and plants. When carbon, nitrogen, phosphorus and sulfur are associated with humus, they become nutrients for both soil microbe activity as well as plant growth.

In nature, humus is constantly introduced into soil as plant debris, dead animals, and other organic matter that decomposes on the ground. Through the alchemy of bacteria, fungi, and other resident micro-life activity, this organic material is reduced by degrees to the soft, spongy essence, called humus. It permeates the top few inches of the soil through rains and the good offices of earthworms and other macro-organisms, where it continually revitalizes the soil around plant roots. This natural cycle is repeated over the seasons out in the wild, sustaining the great forests and other natural areas. Where there is lots of vegetation to decay and enrich the soil, such as in woodland areas, the soil is rich in humus and very fertile. Where there is little or no vegetation to provide the organic debris, such as at the seashore or in the desert, the soil has little or no humus and is lean and infertile.

Soil Fertility

Adding natural ingredients to the soil increases soil microbial activity. Soil microbes fix the nutrients needed for plant growth and release them slowly as plants need them. On the other hand, petrochemical/synthetic fertilizers, insecticides and herbicides are high in soluble salts that are detrimental to microbes and plants alike: they greatly decrease microbial activity and plant uptake. Although these fertilizers are high analysis N-P-K, the plant use efficiency is very low. The plant utilizes only 7-8% of most chemical fertilizers while the rest becomes run-off that can contaminate surface and groundwater.

Natural organic material can be classified into two categories according to their carbon and nitrogen content: Green material and Brown material.

- "Green" materials, such as fresh grass clippings, manure and other living plants (weeds) and plant products contain large amounts of nitrogen.
- "Brown" materials such as dried leaves and plants, branches, and woody materials (leaf stems) have high carbon content but are relatively low in nitrogen.

Basically, "Green" materials supply food for the biolife (bacteria, fungi, and small invertebrates such as worms) which intern manufacture, supply, and facilitate nutrient uptake for the plants. The "Brown" materials provide a home for the "Green" material biolife.

Organic Material and Organic Matter

Organic material is anything that was alive and is now in or on the soil. For it to become organic matter, it must be decomposed into humus. Humus is organic material that has been converted by microorganisms to a resistant state of decomposition. Organic material is unstable in the soil, changing form and mass readily as it decomposes. As much as 90 percent of it disappears quickly because of decomposition providing food and nutrients to biolife. The other 10 percent becomes humus (fertile soil).

What Are the Benefits of Organic Matter?

Nutrient Supply

- Organic matter is a reservoir of nutrients that can be re-leased to the soil. Each percent of organic matter in the soil releases 20 to 30 pounds of nitrogen, 4.5 to 6.6 pounds of P2O5, and 2 to 3 pounds of sulfur per year. The nutrient re-lease occurs predominantly in the spring and summer, so summer crops benefit more from organic-matter mineraliza-tion than winter crops.
- Water-Holding Capacity – Organic matter behaves some-what like a sponge, with the ability to absorb and hold up to 90 percent of its weight in water. A great advantage of the water-holding capacity of organic matter is that the matter will release most of the water that it absorbs to plants. In contrast, clay holds great quantities of water, but much of it is unavailable to plants.
- Soil Structure Aggregation – Organic matter causes soil to clump and form soil aggregates, which improves soil struc-ture. With better soil structure, permeability (infiltration of water through the soil) improves, in turn improving the soil's ability to take up and hold water.
- Erosion Prevention – This property of organic matter is not widely known. Data used in the universal soil loss equation in-dicate that increasing soil organic matter from 1 to 3 per-cent can reduce erosion 20 to 33 percent because of in-creased water infiltration and stable soil aggregate formation caused by organic matter.
- Humus consists of different humic substances:

- o Fulvic acids: the fraction of humus that is soluble in water under all pH conditions. Their color is commonly light yellow to yellow-brown.
- o Humic acids: the fraction of humus that is soluble in water, except for conditions more acid than pH 2. Common colors are dark brown to black.
- Humin: the fraction of humus that is not soluble in water at any pH and that cannot be extracted with a strong base, such as sodium hydroxide (NaOH). Commonly black in color.

The term acid is used to describe humic materials because humus behaves like weak acids.

Non-humic substances: significance and function

Non-humic organic molecules are released directly from cells of fresh residues, such as proteins, amino acids, sugars, and starches. This part of soil organic matter is the active, or easily decomposed, fraction. This active fraction is influenced strongly by weather conditions, moisture status of the soil, growth stage of the vegetation, addition of organic residues, and cultural practices. It is the main food supply for various organisms in the soil.

What to do to build fertile soil for your lawn:

- Mower. Use a soil building organic fertilizer.
- Top-dress your lawn at Recycle your grass and fall leaves with a mulching blade on your least once a year.
- Do not use chemical fertilizers, herbicides, or insecticides. Fertile soil has no need for these.
- Apply a soil amendment rich in humic acid and natural organic substances such as liquid seaweed such as kelp.
- Irrigate your lawn deeply and only when needed. Except for new grass, watering every 10 days or so is sufficient. You can easily determine when to water by observing the stress level of your grass. The roots need the water not the

grass blades. The time to water is when the grass blades start to curl or dry out. Early morning is the best time to water under normal circumstances. Early evening is the most efficient watering time during times of drought.

Centipede Lawn Repair

Instead of allowing bare patches to fill in with weeds, we eliminate them by preparing the soil, replanting grass seed, and properly caring for the area.

Recommended Time for lawn repair

the best time to eliminate bare patches is early spring to early summer before temperatures become too hot.

Grass Seed Selection

To avoid inadvertently planting weeds along with grass, we choose grass seed labeled "certified." Grass seed labeled as certified is inspected for quality and purity, and it contains fewer weed seeds than other varieties. To maintain a uniform appearance, we try to choose grass seed of the same or similar variety to surrounding grass. After mowing a few times, the new grass will eventually blend in with the previously planted variety.

Ground Preparation

There's more to reseeding a bare spot than simply scattering seed over the ground. The ground must be properly prepared, especially if the dead spot is a result of disease. Remove dead grass and remaining live growth, level and properly furrow the area.

Begin by removing all live growth in a partially bare area with a heavy-duty spade, and remove the sod at least six inches beyond the bare area. Remove any rocks and debris, break up large clumps with the tines of a heavy garden rake, work the soil while leveling, and loosen it to a depth of approximately 1/2 inch. If necessary, supplement the existing soil with a fertile loam. Fertile loam is superior in texture, and it's full of essential vitamins and beneficial nutrients.

Furrow the ground by crosshatching vertically and horizontally with a garden rake or a flat-ended shovel. Doing so will help grass seed become embedded within the nooks and crannies of the soil. Seeds scattered on hard flat ground will eventually blow away or end up washing away during the first hard rain.

After the prepared area has been seeded, go over the soil with a light-duty rake to cover the seeds adequately enough to secure them beneath the soil. Straw is sometimes applied for additional protection.

Watering a Newly Seeded Area

Your duty is to lightly water a newly seeded area, and after the seeds are embedded in the soil, water the area at least once a day. Water more often if temperatures are high and during times of excessive wind. The ground should be kept evenly moist but not overly saturated. Once the grass reaches an approximate height of two inches, it should be watered regularly to keep the roots moist and well nourished.

Mowing

Keep pets and children off of newly sown grass, and don't mow until it reaches a height of about three inches. Subsequently strive to maintain a height of about 2 1/2 inches for a beautiful looking healthy lawn.

Why You Should Switch to Organic Lawn Care

Your lawn is safe to play on immediately after application	Pets can roll on the grass, play on the grass, even eat the grass	Safe for people, pets, and the environment.

Biodegradable

- It is safer for humans, pets and the environment than synthetic fertilizers and pesticides.
- It improves the quality of the soil, which will have an increased ability to retain water and nutrients.
- You will enjoy significant financial savings by transitioning from synthetic to organic lawn care, especially after the first year of use.
- Organic products will significantly reduce pests by restoring balance to your lawn's ecosystem. You will benefit from reduced maintenance in mowing, watering and fertilizing because you will have a naturally stronger and healthier lawn.
- A report by the National Academy of Sciences shows that the health of 1 in 7 people is negatively impacted in some form by lawn pesticides.
- Numerous studies link lawn chemicals to cancers and other long-term diseases.
- Several studies also link exposure to artificial lawn chemicals to an increased risk of cancer and other health problems in pets. Children are especially at risk for negative

- Health consequences due to their size, physiological development and proximity to the ground.
- Synthetic pesticides and fertilizers destroy the naturally present beneficial organisms in a healthy lawn's ecosystem. This destruction then transforms your lawn into an increasingly needy "junkie," requiring more and more chemicals to sustain it.
- Organic lawn care focuses instead on soil management techniques and long-term results, building up the nutrients and organisms in the soil in order to make your lawn better able to withstand drought, pests, and other common problems.
- Organic lawn care also eliminates damage to the environment and to human and animal health caused by synthetic lawn care products.
- Organic products function by building up "life in the soil," or soil biology, their payoff is more long-term and lasting.
- Synthetic products, by their nature, are instantaneous and must be frequently reapplied in greater amounts to maintain the appearance of the grass due to the need for frequent reapplications and the reduced effectiveness of synthetic chemicals.
- The user of organic products will spend considerably less money on lawn care over a two-year period than the user of synthetic fertilizers and pesticides.

Top Dressing

100% Bio-enhanced, organic, soil building, top dressing.

- improves soil structure, health, fertility, aeration, compaction, thatch build-up, and weed growth
- reduces water usage by maintaining soil moisture
- reduces rainwater runoff
- lessens soil temperature fluctuations
- reduces maintenance
- eliminates the need for expensive, messy, unproductive mechanical dethatching and aeration
- inhibits many plant diseases
- builds humus
- increases brix values deterring lawn insects
- makes the lawns more attractive

Component	Material	Action
Brown Organic Material	Mulched dry leaves, twigs, dried vegetation, pine needles	Low in nitrogen Trace elements Micro-nutrients Builds humus Brown organic material decomposes into organic matter at a rate of about 5:1 (5 pounds organic material = 1 pound organic matter)
Green Organic Material	Mulched grass clippings, kitchen scraps,	Low in carbon Trace elements Micro-nutrients

		Green organic material de-composes into organic matter at a rate of about 10:1 (10 pounds organic material = 1 pound organic matter)
Composted manure	Composted manure	Adds bulk Adds uniformity Adds micro-macro utrients Adds trace elements Sustains , micro-organisms
Sharp sand	Sharp sand	Adds uniformity
Soil Amenities	Humic acid Kelp Molasses	Plant health Weed control Insect control Increase Brix Disease control

Organic Lawn Care - What to Expect

The Organic Lawn

A lawn, which is cared for correctly and naturally, will eventually begin to take care of itself in many ways. Good soil requires less fertilization, which saves time and money. Organic maintenance practices eliminate imbalances in the soil, which are the initial causes of disease, pest and stress problems in your lawn. By eliminating these causation factors, you eliminate the time and money spent dealing with these types of problems. In the end, you have to look at the big picture. A little extra time and money spent this year will save you a great deal of time and money down the road.

Season One

One of the things that will be happening as you go through your first season on organics is that your lawn may go through "withdrawal" symptoms because of the lack of nitrogen (the intensity of withdrawl systems will be directly affected by the number of years you've applied chemicals, the frequency of previous chemical applications and the typical application rate of those fertilizers).

Chemical fertilizers typically contain about 20 to 35 percent nitrogen. Organic fertilizers will be more like 4 to 10 percent. That is a HUGE drop in nitrogen, and your lawn could go into shock if you don't compensate. You can double the amount of organic fertilizer without causing any harm.

Season Two

Over the next season or two, simply start cutting back on the amount of nitrogen you're applying. As the soil is built up by use of organic fertilizers and soil amendments, the lawn will require less and less nitrogen.

Depending upon how long you've been using chemical fertilizer and how much you've been using, this process may take longer or may go much more quickly than is outlined above.

Organic methods tend to expose imbalances in the soil and other detrimental situations that chemical fertilizers hide (and generally make worse) and correct them. Soil compaction, weeds, insects, disease, drainage, Brix, and above all Humus.

By implementing a solid natural/organic lawncare program, you should be looking at a very healthy, chemical free lawn within about a season or two, maybe three if your lawn is in really bad shape.

Dangers of Synthetic/Chemical Fertilizers, Insecticides, and Herbicides

Chemical fertilizers, herbicides and pesticides poison our waters, our soils, other living creatures and our own bodies.

Herbicides

While most modern herbicides are designed to kill only plants and have little or no toxicity to humans, many still have extreme consequences in the environment, changing habitats in ways that affect insects and wildlife. These consequences extend to watercourses where they may kill beneficial aquatic plants and fish.

Researchers have discovered a group of fungi that protect lawn grasses from pests. The fungi is called endophytes and live in a symbiotic relationship that benefits both plant and fungus. The fungi produce a toxin that are harmless to the grass (and humans) but repels chinch bugs, sod webworms and other surface feeding insects.

Inorganic Fertilizer

The overuse of chemical or inorganic fertilizers has serious consequences including the leaching of nitrates into the ground water supply and the introduction of certain contaminants, Found in synthetic fertilizers, including cadmium, into the soils. Fertilizer run-off into ponds, lakes and streams over stimulates algae growth, suffocating other aquatic plants, invertebrates and fish. Toxic fertilizers made from industrial waste can bring mercury, lead and arsenic to our soil and water supplies.

Pesticides

By far, the most damage to the environment and the biggest threat to our health come from pesticides. It is becoming harder and harder to justify their widespread use. We now know that pesticides are not as effective as claimed and that they cause more harm than good.

It has been estimated that there are 930 Billion microorganisms in each 1 pound of soil under grass turf (Eliot Roberts of the Lawn Institute)!

Note: Less than 1% of the insects in the world are considered pests. The other 99% play an integral role in the ecosystem. Pesticides harm the 99% beneficial insects also.

All of the dozen or so commonly recommended lawn pesticides are suspected of causing serious long term health problems. Captan and Benomyl are carcinogens and mutagens. Many people have severe allergic reactions to Captan often requiring hospitalization. Dursban has caused chronic kidney damage in laboratory tests and 2,4D has been linked to lymphatic cancer. Many homeowners report problems with common lawn chemicals causing excruciating headaches, nausea, extreme fatigue, and other debilitating illnesses. Garbage Magazine, July/August 1990.

A study reported in the "American Journal of Public Health" has found that children whose yards were treated with herbicides (weed & feed) and insecticides had four times the risk of certain cancers. Houston Chronicle, February 27, 1995.

- The National Academy of Science has said "exposures to pesticides early in life can lead to a greater risk of... cancer, neurodevelopment impairment, and immune dysfunction". This means our children are in far greater danger.

- A medical school study shows that children in families that use a lot of pesticides are nearly seven times as likely to develop leukemia. .....The EPA estimates that 300,000 hired farm workers and their children suffer acute illness and injuries from exposure to pesticides each year. Farm Workers Still Unprotected, New York Times 2/25/92.

Natural Weed Control

Natural weed control in Centipede grass is easier than in most warm season grasses. Most broadleaf weeds do poorly in low pH soils (below 7.0) and Centipede's ideal pH condition is a pH 4.5 to 6.5. Adding iron and or sulfur not only lowers pH and controls weeds but also has a greening effect on the grass.

Most natural weed killers available in stores are based on herbal solutions. Many utilize corn gluten, which is a natural substance that inhibits growth of weeds by stopping seed germination. The N-P-P (nitrogen – phosphorus – potassium) designation for corn gluten is 9-0-0. Phosphorus harms the roots of Centipede grass and potassium is handled poorly by it so corn gluten is an ideal weed control for it. Application in the fall stops weeds over the winter (many weeds are not dormant then) and an application in late spring protects the lawn during the summer.

Weedy lawns are often the results of poor drainage and compaction! Aerifying the lawn in the spring solves these conditions. I have found a liquid aerifying agent is far more effective than mechanical aeration and is less expensive with a lot less mess.

Weeds are direct sun lovers but grow close to the ground. Cutting your Centipede grass at 2" to 2-1/2" lets the blades shade the weeds further deterring their growth and spread. Grass root depth is directly related to grass height. 2-inch grass will have 2-inch deep roots. Healthy Centipede turf covers the ground so effectively that weeds simply do not have enough light, or space to grow.

Good organic lawn care involves more than fertilizer and avoiding pesticides. It means building up your lawn's root structure and the soil that supports it so that you achieve a natural balance. Organic techniques that balance will last forever!

Four Step Organic Lawn Program

Our Organic 4-Step DIY Program for Centipede Lawns

Below is a summary of our 4-Step Liquid Organic Law Program for Centipede lawns.

Early spring

For your convenience, we have pre-mixed the optimum springtime nutrient package for the Centipede lawn.

50% Liquid Corn Gluten Meal. This biofertilizer combines the effectiveness of Corn Gluten Meal (CGM) with the convenience of a spray able liquid material. Effective as a pre-emergent for crabgrass and many broadleaf weeds, yet lower nitrogen than granular forms to help you more effectively manage your turf nitrogen budget. Our exclusive formulation results from enzymatic hydrolysis of CGM and addition of a liquid carrier to provide a convenient, economical organic pre-emergent product.

9.38% biological dethatcher. Biological Dethatcher is a liquid solution that has been formulated to generate and accelerate the decomposition of thatch in lawns. To fuel this process, this product contains high levels of thatch digesting Bacteria and Enzymes killed off by chemical and synthetic fertilizers. These, along with naturally occurring soil organisms, will break down thatch and turn it into valuable humus very quickly making for a plush healthy lawn.

40.61% Liquid Iron. Liquid iron in a chelated formula makes iron available to plants even in highly acidic soil. Iron makes for healthy, dark green growth. Iron is essential for photosynthesis. Iron is necessary for chlorophyll formation and, without it; plants would not be able to carry out essential cellular functions.

0.01% Dechlorinator. Chlorine is harmful to biolife (bacteria, fungi, and enzymes), because nearly all municipal water supplies are chlori-nated, we add this to all our bioactive products.

Springtime Centipede lawn nutrient package

Quart	$8.25	Coverage 2,200 sq. ft.
½ Gallon	$13.25	Coverage 4,400 sq. ft.
Gallon	$21.00	Coverage 8,800 sq. ft.

Late spring

For your convenience, we have pre-mixed the optimum late spring nutrient package for the Centipede lawn.

49.99% liquid aerifying agent. A soil penetrant that breaks apart tightly bonded compacted particles. This creates "space" in the soil, allowing roots, water and oxygen to permeate. Once you get oxygen into a compacted soil, beneficial microbes will be able to survive and turn organic matter into all-important humus. When you have humus, you will have much better soil quality and structure.

0.01% Dechlorinator. Chlorine is harmful to biolife (bacteria, fungi, and enzymes), because nearly all municipal water supplies are chlorinated, we add this to all our bioactive products.

This:

- Eliminates the need for mechanical aeration * see below
- Reduces soil compaction
- Breaks up clay deeply
- Improves soil structure and humus formation
- Increases earthworm activity
- Helps bioactivate all soils

- Safe to use around sprinklers
- Improves rooting by loosening soil
- Improves air and water penetration
- Is an IONIZED Soil Conditioner
- Is completely biodegradable
- Helps save water & reduce plant stress and disease
- Improves drainage & prevents erosion

50% blend of two of the best soil activators and plant health products in the world: Humic Acid (often called liquid humus) and Seaweed (kelp). It serves three major functions that result in better soil and plant health:

- It helps detoxify and buffer chemicals and salts that prevent bioactivity in the soil.
- One Gallon of our Humic Acid is equivalent to 7 tons of manure
- It helps generate the soil-improving microbes necessary for good soil structure, bioactivity and plant health.
- It provides numerous plant trace nutrients and biostimulants.

The Humic Acid in Soil Activator is a full 17% solution, the highest level we know of. If you check other liquid humic acid products, you will find they will not exceed 12% strength. One gallon of our Humic Acid is equivalent to 7 tons of manure in terms of soil bioactivation. We also use a superior grade Seaweed - Ascophylum Nodosum, grown and harvested off the coast of Norway. We also add some Blackstrap Molasses as an energy source for biolife. We believe this is the best soil activator on the market.

Here are just some of the many benefits of this blend.

- Bioactivates both clay and sandy soils and increases organic matter
- Buffers harsh chemical salts or chlorides found in many commercial fertilizers

- Provides carbon which feeds beneficial soil microbes
- Improves soil structure and aeration
- Stimulates root growth and supports most plant functions
- Unlocks and chelates major and minor nutrients. Reduces fertilizer needs.
- Improves plant's ability to capture (fix) atmospheric nitrogen
- Prevents Thatch buildup and helps stimulate the decomposition of existing Thatch
- Increases earthworm activity
- Makes iron and other nutrients more available in poor pH soils
- Improves plant resistance to disease, insects and other stress
- Supplies over 30 micro-nutrients and vitamins
- Works as a catalyst for both soil regeneration and plant growth
- Contains 58.2% Humic Acid and 41.8% Seaweed

Late Spring Centipede lawn nutrient package

Quart	$17.00	Coverage	4.000 sq. ft.
½ Gallon	$27.50	Coverage	8.000 sq. ft.
Gallon	$44.00	Coverage	16.000 sq. ft.

Summer

37.5% blend of two of the best soil activators and plant health products in the world: Humic Acid (often called liquid humus) and Seaweed (kelp). It serves three major functions that result in better soil and plant health:

- It helps detoxify and buffer chemicals and salts that prevent bioactivity in the soil.
- It helps generate the soil-improving microbes necessary for good soil structure, bioactivity and plant health.

- It provides numerous plant trace nutrients and biostimulants.

The Humic Acid in our blend is a full 17% solution, the highest level we know of. If you check other liquid humic acid products, you will find they will not exceed 12% strength. One gallon of our Humic Acid is equivalent to 7 tons of manure in terms of soil bioactivation. We also use a superior grade Seaweed - Ascophylum Nodosum, grown and harvested off the coast of Norway. We also add some Blackstrap Molasses as an energy source for biolife. We believe this is the best soil activator on the market.

Here are just some of the many benefits of this blend.

- Bioactivates both clay and sandy soils and increases Organic Matter
- Buffers harsh chemical salts or chlorides found in many commercial fertilizers
- Provides carbon which feeds beneficial soil microbes
- Improves soil structure and aeration Stimulates root growth and supports most plant functions
- Unlocks and chelates major and minor nutrients. Reduces fertilizer needs.
- Improves plant's ability to capture (fix) atmospheric nitrogen
- Prevents Thatch buildup and helps stimulate the decomposition of existing Thatch
- Increases earthworm activity
- Makes iron and other nutrients more available in poor pH soils
- Improves plant resistance to disease, insects and other stress
- Supplies over 30 micro-nutrients and vitamins
- Works as a catalyst for both soil regeneration and plant growth
- Contains 58.2% Humic Acid and 41.8% Seaweed

62.5% Liquid Sulfur. The sulfur slowly breaks down (with help from oxygen from the air and water) to produce an acid that lowers the pH of the soil. The lower pH of the soil helps make the iron naturally in the soil more available to the grass as a nutrient. Iron helps provide a deep green color.

Summer Centipede lawn nutrient package

Quart	$5.50	Coverage 2,000 sq. ft.
½ Gallon	$8.50	Coverage 4,000 sq. ft.
Gallon	$13.50	Coverage 8,000 sq. ft.

Fall

71.20% Liquid Corn Gluten Meal. This biofertilizer combines the effectiveness of Corn Gluten Meal (CGM) with the convenience of a spray able liquid material. Effective as

- A pre-emergent for crabgrass and many broadleaf weeds, yet lower nitrogen than granular forms to help you more effec-tively manage your turf nitrogen budget. Our exclusive formulation results from enzymatic hydrolysis of CGM and addition of a liquid carrier to provide a convenient, economical organic pre-emergent product.

28.20% blend of two of the best soil activators and plant health products in the world: Humic Acid (often called liquid humus) and Seaweed (kelp). It serves three major functions that result in better soil and plant health:

- It helps detoxify and buffer chemicals and salts that prevent bioactivity in the soil.
- It helps generate the soil-improving microbes necessary for good soil structure, bioactivity and plant health.

- It provides numerous plant trace nutrients and biostimulants.
- The Humic Acid in Nature's Magic is a full 17% solution, the highest level we know of. If you check other liquid humic acid products, you will find they will not exceed 12% strength. One gallon of our Humic Acid is equivalent to 7 tons of manure in terms of soil bioactivation. We also use a superior grade Seaweed - Ascophylum Nodosum, grown and harvested off the coast of Norway. We also add some Blackstrap Molasses as an energy source for biolife. We believe this is the best soil activator on the market.

Here are just some of the many benefits of this blend.

- Bioactivates both clay and sandy soils and increases organic matter
- Buffers harsh chemical salts or chlorides found in many commercial fertilizers
- Provides carbon which feeds beneficial soil microbes Improves soil structure and aeration
- Stimulates root growth and supports most plant functions
- Unlocks and chelates major and minor nutrients.
- Reduces fertilizer needs.
- Improves plant's ability to capture (fix) atmospheric nitrogen
- Prevents thatch buildup and helps stimulate the decomposition of existing thatch
- Increases earthworm activity
- Makes iron and other nutrients more available in poor pH soils
- Improves plant resistance to disease, insects and other stress
- Supplies over 30 micro-nutrients and vitamins
- Works as a catalyst for both soil regeneration and plant growth
- Works as a catalyst for both soil regeneration and plant growth
- Contains 58.2% Humic Acid and 41.8% Seaweed

Fall Centipede lawn nutrient package

Quart $8.25   Coverage 2,200 sq. ft.

½ Gallon $13.25   Coverage 4,400 sq. ft.

Gallon $21.00   Coverage 8,800 sq. ft.

How to Use Hose End Sprayers

How to Use a Hose-end Sprayer

Hose-end sprayers are a great tool for spraying liquid garden and lawn products. You need to know a little bit about how they work or you will undoubtedly have a problem with over or under-applying your products.

Hose End Sprayer

Available at Lowe's

Hose-end sprayer application is very simple. You have a spray head applicator that screws onto both the top of a bottle and onto your garden hose. A small hole has been made underneath the spray head, and a siphon tube is snugly connected over this hole. The siphon tube goes into the bottle, which contains the liquid product.

When you turn the sprayer on, water passes through the spray head on top of the bottle and shoots out the other end. As the water moves through the top of the spray head, it creates suction or vacuum that siphons the liquid product up the tube to the top of the spray head. There, and not in the bottle, it mixes with the hose water and is sprayed out. Most hose-end sprayers have a knob or button that allows you to close off the hole on the siphon tube so you can spray water only if desired.

The size of the hole underneath the spray head will determine how many ounces (or teaspoons) of liquid product is to be siphoned up for every gallon of water that you spray. Sprayers will have either just one hole underneath, or they will have multiple holes (or settings) that you can utilize.

Adjustable hose-end sprayers have a dial on top that allows you to choose from multiple hole sizes, ranging from as low as 1 tea-spoon per gallon to 8 oz per gallon.

Pre-set or Fixed Rate sprayers are usually found on RTU (Ready-To-Use) products. There is just one hole in the spray head so it always siphons out at the same rate. The only way to change the rate of siphoning would be to put reducer-tip at the end of the siphon tube.

APPLYING THE CORRECT AMOUNT OF YOUR PRODUCT

Most garden product labels will recommend applying a certain amount of the product per every 1000 sf. But all hose-end spray-ers are set up to siphon out in ounces per gallon- not ounces per 1000 sf. So, how do you go about getting the right amount of ounces per 1000 sq. ft. applied?

The key fact you need to know about hose-end sprayers is this:

- The amount of product that gets sprayed out on a lawn is determined by both the sprayer hole (oz per gal) setting, and by how many gallons of water you actually spray on the lawn as you do an application. Moreover, because every-one walks at a different speed, sprays a wider or narrower swath and has different water pressure, there is always going to be some trial and error when using a hose-end sprayer.

- Here is our advice on how to apply products with either a fixed rate sprayer or an adjustable hose-end sprayer :
- Before you start spraying, get an approximate idea of the total area (in square feet) that is going to be sprayed. Walk it off heel-to-toe if necessary and measure length and width to get the area. Multiply the length x width to get the total area, figure out how much of the product you should use. For example, if your yard is 4,000 sf and you want to apply a product at 4 oz per 1000 sq. ft. rate, you want to use 16 oz total on your lawn.
- Attach your garden hose to the sprayer. Turn your water on at about ½ to ¾ pressures for best functioning of the sprayer. You can turn the sprayer to the Water Only setting while you get the pressure right.
- If you are using a fixed rate sprayer, turn the sprayer to ON (MIX). If you are using an adjustable sprayer, set it to 1 oz per gallon. Walk at a slow to normal pace moving your wrist side to side enough to spray a 6'-8' wide swath over the lawn (or gardens). Spray enough to make sure all areas get wet on top. You do not have to soak these areas at this time. You can water it in later.
- After you have sprayed a small area, say ¼ or ½ of the lawn stop and check to see how much of the product you have used up. Figure out if you have sprayed too much or too little based on how much area has been treated. For example, if you have treated about 2000 sf and you want to apply at 4 oz per 1000 sf, you should have used approximately 8 oz (or 1 cup) of the product.

If you have used too little, you need to walk at a slower pace when spraying and/or spray a narrower swath. If you are using an adjustable sprayer you can simply increase the spray setting and walk exactly like you did the first time. Test another area re-adjust as needed.

If you have used too much, you need to walk faster and/or spray a wider swath. If you are using an adjustable sprayer you can turn it down to a lower setting.

If nothing or very little has come out of the sprayer check to see that the siphon tube is still connected. If there is a filter tip on the end of the tube, make sure it is not clogged (soaking it in club soda will remove clogs).

As we said, there is always some trial and error when you spray with a hose-end sprayer. Even commercial lawn spray technicians have practice and make adjustments to get their walking speed and spray pattern down correctly. It gets easier after you have done it once or twice.

For shipping information and costs, contact us at information@swstout.com.

We accept major credit cards through PayPal

Glossary

Acid: An acid (from the Latin acidus meaning sour) is traditionally considered any chemical compound that, when dissolved in water, gives a solution with a hydrogen ion activity greater than in pure water, i.e. a pH less than 7.0.

Aeration: Aerating a lawn means supplying the soil with air while helping water and nutrients move into the root zone.

Amino acids: Amino acids play central roles both as building blocks of proteins and as intermediates in metabolism.

Auxins: Auxins have an essential role in coordination of many growth and behavioral processes in the plant life cycle.

Base: Any chemical compound that, when dissolved in water, gives a solution with a hydrogen ion activity lower than that of pure water, i.e. a pH higher than 7.0 at standard conditions.

Beneficial Nematodes: Beneficial nematodes are under-ground pest hunters that control over 250 different species of insects that spend some part of their lives underground. They are a very efficient organic insect control method and kill most insects before they become adults.

Brix: Brix refers to the total soluble solids (TSS) in the juice of the produce or sap of the plant. Total soluble solids refer not only to sucrose (sugar) but also to fructose, vitamins, minerals, amino acids, proteins, hormones, and other solids.

Brown Organic Material: "Brown" materials such as dried leaves and plants, branches, and woody materials (leaf stems) have high carbon content but are relatively low in nitrogen.

Centipede Decline: In mature Centipede grass lawns (3 or more years old) problem areas sometimes appear in the spring and grow worse throughout the summer. These problem areas usually develop in thatchy turf, compacted soils, drought areas or areas under other stresses. Since a specific disease organism has not been identified as the cause, the problem has been broadly named "Centipede decline"

Chelated: Chelated minerals are specially formulated mineral supplements designed to improve absorption of these essential nutrients into the tissues.

Decomposition: Decomposition refers to the process by which tissues of a dead organism break down into simpler forms of matter. Such a breakdown of dead organisms is essential for new growth and development of living organisms because it recycles the finite matter that occupies physical space in the soil.

Drought Stress: Prolonged drought stress to plants is unhealthy and predisposes them to pest problems. A plant under drought stress is in a weakened state and its defenses are low. Insects and diseases take advantage of the situation and add to the plants' stress.

Enzymes: Enzymes are very efficient catalysts for bio-chemical reactions. They speed up reactions by providing an alternative reaction pathway of lower activation energy.

Fulvic Acids: Fulvic acids: the fraction of humus that is soluble in water under all pH conditions. Their color is commonly light yellow to yellow-brown.

Fungicides: Fungicides are chemical compounds or biological organisms used to kill or inhibit fungi or fungal spores.

Gibberellins: Gibberellins (GAs) are plant hormones that regulate growth and influence various developmental processes, including stem elongation, germination, dormancy, flowering, sex expression, enzyme induction, and leaf and fruit senescence.

Green Organic Material: "Green materials", such as fresh grass clippings, manure and other living plants (weeds) and plant products contain large amounts of nitrogen.

Groundwater Contamination: Groundwater contamination occurs when man-made products such as synthetic fertilizers, gasoline, oil, road salts and chemicals get into the groundwater and cause it to become unsafe and unfit for human use.

Herbicides: A herbicide is a substance used to kill unwanted plants. Selective herbicides kill specific targets while leaving the desired crop relatively unharmed. Some of these act by interfering with the growth of the weed and are often synthetic "imitations" of plant hormones. Herbicides used to clear waste ground, industrial sites, railways and railway embankments are non-selective and kill all plant material with which they come into contact.

Humic Acids: Humic Acid promotes deeper rooting, multiplies nutrient uptake and unlocks nutrients normally tied up in the soil. It also energizes plants like no other material on earth.

Humin: A black humic substance that is not soluble in water.

Humus: Humus refers to any organic matter that has reached a point of stability, where it will break down no further and might, if conditions do not change, remain essentially as it is for centuries, if not millennia. Humus is fertile soil.

Insecticides: An insecticide is a pesticide used against insects. They include ovicides and parricides used against the eggs and larvae of insects respectively. Insecticides are used in agriculture, medicine, industry and the household. The use of insecticides is believed to be one of the major factors behind the increase in agricultural productivity in the 20th century. Nearly all insecticides have the potential to significantly alter ecosystems; many are toxic to humans; and others are concentrated in the food chain.

Indoles: Indoles are hormones that promote the development of roots in plant cuttings.

Micronutrients: Micronutrients are those elements essential for plant growth which are needed in only very small (micro) quantities . These elements are sometimes called minor elements or trace elements, but use of the term micronutrient is encouraged by the American Society of Agronomy and the Soil Science Society of America. The micronutrients are boron (B), copper (Cu), iron (Fe), chloride (Cl), manganese (Mn), molybdenum (Mo) and zinc (Zn). Recycling organic matter such as grass clippings and tree leaves is an excellent way of providing micronutrients (as well as macro-nutrients) to growing plants.

Non-humic Substances: Non-humic substances are all those materials that can be placed in one of the categories of discrete compounds such as sugars, amino acids, fats and so on.

Nutrients: A nutrient is a chemical that an organism needs to live and grow or a substance used in an organ-ism's metabolism which must be taken in from its environment.

Organic lawn care: Organic lawn care focuses instead on soil management techniques and long-term results, building up the nutrients and organisms in the soil in order to make your lawn better able to withstand drought, pests, and other common problems.

Organic matter: Application of organic matter to the soil adds carbon, which promotes the growth of beneficial bacteria, which increases the likelihood of hearty plants. Another benefit is when crops grow and demand more nutrients; added organic matter can be used as plant food. Remember that every time you disturb soil by turning or tilling, oxygen also is added to the soil. This increas-es microbial activity, which feeds on organic matter. Therefore, soil disturbance can decrease the soil's organic matter reserves and should be kept to a minimum.

pH: pH is a measure of the acidity or basicity of a solution.

Pesticides: A pesticide may be a chemical substance, biological agent (such as a virus or bacteria), antimicrobial-al, disinfectant or device used against any pest. Pests include insects, plant pathogens, weeds, mollusks, birds, mammals, fish, nematodes (roundworms), microbes and people that destroy property, spread or are a vector for disease or cause a nuisance. Although there are benefits to the use of pesticides, there are also drawbacks, such as potential toxicity to humans and other animals.

Proteins: Proteins (also known as polypeptides) are organic compounds made of amino acids arranged in a linear chain and folded into a globular form.

Rhizomes: In botany, a rhizome is a characteristically horizontal stem of a plant that is usually found under-ground, often sending out roots and shoots from its nodes. Rhizomes may also be referred to as creeping rootstalks, or rootstocks.

Secondary Macronutrients: Secondary Macronutrients are also known as micronutrients.

Senescence: Senescence refers to the biological changes which take place in organisms as they age.

Soil compaction: Soil compaction occurs when the weight of livestock or heavy machinery compresses the soil, causing it to lose pore space. Soil compaction may also occur due to a lack of water in the soil. Affected soils become less able to absorb rainfall, thus increasing runoff and erosion. Plants have difficulty in compacted soil because the mineral grains are pressed together, leaving little space for air and water, which are essential for root growth. Burrowing animals also find a hostile environment, because the denser soil is more difficult to penetrate.

Soil microbes: There are in a healthy soil literally hundreds and hundreds of species of soil bacteria, soil fungi, and many other microscopic soil critters. A single tablespoon of healthy soil might contain over a billion beneficial soil microbes!!! The problem is that most of the soils in the home landscapes of America have a very low population of these valuable and important soil microbes due to prolonged use of synthetic fertilizers, herbicides, and insecticides.

Soil structure: Soil structure is determined by how individual soil granules clump or bind together and aggregate, and therefore, the arrangement of soil pores between them. Soil structure has a major influence on water and air movement, biological activity, root growth and seedling emergence.

Sting Nematodes: The sting nematode is a microscopic roundworm averaging about 1/12 inch in length. It is found almost exclusively in soils with a sand content of 80 percent or higher and thrives best in irrigated cropland where there is a constant supply of moisture. Sting nematodes do not enter plant roots'. All life stages remain in the soil, feeding at or near root tips. Even small populations can cause serious damage because of a powerful toxic chemical injected into the roots during feeding.

Stolons: In botany, stems which grow at the soil surface or below ground form new plants at the ends or at the nodes. Stolons are often called runners. Imprecisely they are stems that run atop or just under the ground; more specifically, a stolon is a horizontal shoot from a plant that grows on top of or below the soil surface with the ability to produce new clones of the same plant from buds at the tip

Symbiotic bacteria: Symbiotic bacteria are able to live in or on plant or animal tissue. In digestive systems, symbiotic bacteria help break down foods that contain fiber. They also help produce vitamins.

Synthetic Fertilizers: Synthetic just means "man made." The elements (nitrogen, potassium and phosphorus) are still there, but have been bonded with other com-pounds or carriers (such as salts). High concentrations of salts that can over time, damage grass plants and ad-adversely affect the composition of the soil.

Thatch: Thatch in lawns is often misunderstood; both its cause and control. Some lawns have serious thatch problems while others do not. Thatch is a layer of living and dead organic matter that occurs between the green matter and the soil surface. Excessive thatch (over 1/2 inch thick) creates a favorable environment for pests and disease, an unfavorable growing environment for grass roots, and can interfere with some lawn care practices.

Vitamins: A vitamin is an organic compound required as a nutrient in tiny amounts by an organism. A compound is called a vitamin when it cannot be synthesized in sufficient quantities by an organism, and must be obtained from the diet.

INDEX

Made in the USA
Columbia, SC
29 September 2017